GLOBAL PEACEFUL HUMAN DEVELOPMENT AND DESIGN

Elizabeth Wiley MA JD, Pomo Elder

Order this book online at www.trafford.com
or email orders@trafford.com

Most Trafford titles are also available at major online book retailers.

 www.trafford.com

North America & international
toll-free: 844 688 6899 (USA & Canada)
fax: 812 355 4082

Our mission is to efficiently provide the world's finest, most comprehensive book publishing
service, enabling every author to experience success. To find out how to publish your book,
your way, and have it available worldwide, visit us online at www.trafford.com

Because of the dynamic nature of the Internet, any web addresses or links contained in this book may have changed since publication and may no longer be valid. The views expressed in this work are solely those of the author and do not necessarily reflect the views of the publisher, and the publisher hereby disclaims any responsibility for them.

Any people depicted in stock imagery provided by Getty Images are models,
and such images are being used for illustrative purposes only.
Certain stock imagery © Getty Images.

ISBN: 978-1-6987-1360-1 (sc)
ISBN: 978-1-6987-1359-5 (e)

Library of Congress Control Number: 2022918554

Print information available on the last page.

Trafford rev. 12/07/2022

GLOBAL PEACEFUL HUMAN DEVELOPMENT AND DESIGN

Global world peace. my Dad (RIP Dad) went to war (WWII, lied about his age, and got his Mom to sign because the recruiters said it was the war to end war, and as a California Native American he wanted to be part of peace forever on earth, (no folks California was NOT empty of humans before the gold greed dash in the mid 1800's....as a friend from another country told me they learned in his COLLEGE) and NO, not bush bunnies waiting for the "civilized" armies of Cortez to come free us, or move everyone to the concentration camps where families were torn apart forever, children had white hot cattle branding tools shoved on their tongues, if caught speaking their native languages, as we all learned in school in America and create a life in heaven for them, working as slaves in homes and businesses of those who invaded their countries with newly invented guns. (Google 1492 and Columbus use of firearms against Native nations).

The Native California people are now proven to have had irrigation, set cities, legal and education systems before the Cortez genocide squads arrived) My Dad thought ending war forever was something he wanted to be part of, instead as a top ranked sharp shooter, and "expendable" with a military ID card that stated on the back "it is a federal offense to provide alcohol to aborigines"...... being shot after being parachuted behind enemy lines to keep the Nazi troops from doubling back on D Day, or from getting supplies from the rear, he was just abandoned, along with other "expendables" dropped by "expendable" pilots in old planes (guess the planes and pilots were "expendable" as well. I HAVE FELT a lifelong commitment to demanding that world peace, END TO WAR, my Dad was promised. PEACE ON EARTH. RIP

Dad and all other "expendables" My Dad told me what war is.....it is two young people face to face, one better get the draw and kill the other, or be murdered for something some old fart somewhere wants that is NOT their right. My Dad told me an ancient Native belief, which is that murdering unarmed people, especially Elders, women and children is GENOCIDE. I feel heart felt, and God felt that means we need Peace on earth. Whether a criminal, or a politician, no one should kill, or be killed by armed others fighting somehow "instead" of the person behind it all. As Bob Dylan pointed out, they ALL claimed God on Our Side. I do not believe God, Creator of ALL tells us, or wants us to use His presence to justify anyone killing anyone else. RIP Dad. Live in peace the rest of us.....in memory of the billions who have died since the first caveman picked up a rock and hit someone else on the head so as to NOT work for a living. Of Course, with God on his side!

One day, I just thought and this picture came to mind. A caveman somewhere, not having found enough food, threw a rock at a prey animal or bird, hit a person, who had prey in hand, by accident, and crime started. That person found stooges to go out an hit others with prey with rocks and racketeering crime was invented, and then a group began to gather rocks to sell to big groups of those who by flapping leather flags and singing patriotic songs got to go steal game and gathered plants for the one "leader" and genocide was born. Another leader and rock gathering/selling gang grew up and "civilization", as well as WAR was born.

Thats their story and they are sticking to it, with drones and missiles and taxpayer funds.

DONA NOBIS PACEM

While Latin, many people learned this piece of music, and as a chant, song, or part of a religious service, people have asked God for peace.

Look this up on You Tube.

It appears to be disputed as to who put the music to the simple words, yet Mozart is given credit for the major Canon.

As a child, attending the "Winter Skies" show at the Griffith Park Observatory in Los Angeles, CA, we were told that research had shown that every religion, quasi religious and against religions group for centuries had celebrated the Winter Stars, and asked for peace on earth.

Global Peaceful Human Development and Design

Phases:

1. Self
2. Family
3. Friends/neighbors
4. City
5. County
6. State

7. Nation
8. International
9. Global

Each of us can learn about all the phases while working on ONE phase. Self. Having peace IN YOURSELF is the first step, however while working on that step, you can and need to expand beyond yourself to attain that peace in yourself. Working on yourself is an open ended category, if we stay open and growing, we become more peaceful within and have more peace to share in other categories.

Global Peaceful Human Development and Design

Phases: Each of these phases can be worked on together, one by one, or all nine at once, but until you find peace within yourself, it will be easier to learn, live, or teach any other person peace.

1. Self
2. Family
3. Friends/neighbors
4. City
5. County
6. State
7. Nation
8. International
9. Global

SELF: LEARN TO BE AT PEACE WITH MYSELF.

From early in each of our lives, we start the first lack of peace in our own lives. Most start life with a cry, a whine and complaint.

We wake up in the morning with a dispute over getting up, daily personal care, whether to go to school, or work today, and how and why to involve others in our day.

This is a lot of internal disorder to address before getting out of bed.

It is a lot of internal stress before we see one other person in our day.

Children do not want to eat, or wear what is expected. They do not want to go to school. They have already started the day saying they do not want to get up.

There are many positive child rearing programs to facilitate your child being able to deal with the reality that each of us learns to determine these choices and make them work for ourselves. The best of these programs help YOU to allow your child to make choices and pay the consequences for bad choices. The worst and some mediocre programs will leave your child in a lot of pain in life, fighting with themselves and everyone else. Possibly spending a lot of money on therapy or worse, jail, addictions and blaming everyone else for that reality.

These child raising programs are adjusted for adults to look back and see where they learned sad, bad, and heartbreaking ways to "deal" with reality.

In the Success Principles from Jack Canfield you can find exercises that will help you identify what you would have changed about your own upbringing that has left you limiting yourself in life. This does NOT mean let your six year old go on dates, or buying your sixteen year old a $100,000 sports car which will ruin THEIR lives. As a Certified Level One Canfield Success Principles trainer, I would get this book, and read it, cover to cover. Second, read use markers and pens and put tabs on pages special to YOU. In your third read, start at the beginning and DO the exercises. Find the Canfield website and sign up for free introductory classes and LEARN who YOU really are, and what YOU really want, not what someone else wanted you to be (usually not a bother and get money to help them out). Not what commercials or "trendy" ads and movies, or books wanted you to be.

Most of us have to pay the rent, so create a timeline and daily schedule to make sure you have time to find YOU and build YOU as YOU want to be. Get a job that will pay the rent, but leave YOU time to enjoy building your own life.

I met a client online from a third world country who had wanted to play football, all his life. He was still young, but not young enough to go find a high school, or college and become a world famous football star. Yet, I said, think about this, do you even play football. The answer was no. He had never held a football in his hands. He discovered what he "dreamed" of was being rich and doing all the things he saw rich, famous athletes do in movies and on television. As he went through his process, he found a local (no cars, no busses in that area) church program for abandoned children and orphans. He got accepted to have the older boys help him build a dirt lot football field. No bulldozers, they raked and shoveled and leveled and marked the field by hand.

On his group went, using his phone from his pay the rent job. They wrote to football teams all over the world with pictures and texts of what they were doing and asked for donations of equipment and clothing. College and high school teams began to help them. As time passed, he began to learn football from training books and videos people shared with him.

At one point he found others, and helped them build their own dirt lot football fields at other third world schools and start their own football league. Many of those who helped them came to visit and help them learn. Most found out that being an athlete was hard and daily WORK. Yet, as time has passed the original dream of being a world famous football player came true in a way as the coach kept helping others start similar programs and some of his players were scouted by high school and college teams that helped them with education as well.

The point of this story is based on a story I saw on a religious television ministry about a group who wanted to start theatre group. They too used shovels, brooms and rakes and leveled out a theatre. They found a few thrown away steel fence posts and raised money to buy a few bags of concrete, set the fence posts with heavy wire they also found at the dump which made up their "stage". Finding old chairs and couches they created a tiered audience seating and started their own theatre. A ballet group had inspired them. A few towns away mirrors set into frames and a sand dance floor helped the dancers learn to dance. They built their exercise barre around the edges of the sand from materials found at the dump.

Yesterday I was clever, and wanted to change the world, today I am wise, and have learned to change myself—-RUMI

All of the hate and blame, bitterness and anger we carry around limits us. In this part of Global Peaceful Human Development and Design, learn to make peace with it all, the past is gone the future not here, live now, find what YOU are and want to be. Find YOUR path. Love, care, and peace will be greater on earth. God bless.

FAMILY: MAKING PEACE AT HEART AND AT HOME

What is family?

Family is your home, and your heart people that frame, and have helped to establish your relationships and how you relate to consistent people.

In the past, and in some areas of the world families were huge numbers of blood related people. Today many people are orphans, adopted, foster children, or have only one or two siblings. Due to marriage, divorce and remarriage step-relations often outnumber blood relations. In many areas and cultures family relationships are set in solid stone of tradition.

Many Americans, among others, have only one, or no child families. People grow and build family with many along the way. Family is for many those who you absolutely KNOW you can trust, and they can trust you. To love, care, and be honest and stand up to each other when necessary.

How do we find what kind of relationships formed and framed us?

How do we figure out if we want to continue those patterns?

How do we get along with those we live with in a more positive and better relationship method than how we grew up?

Do we want to?

There is an old saying about leading a horse to water. You can not make a horse drink because YOU think it needs water. No one can MAKE you have a happier, more joyful, more caring life by telling you how to do it, or showing you ways to achieve that better, happier, more joyful and caring life. YOU have to decide you are thirsty enough to find water, and drink it.

There is another old saying, one shared in Jack Canfield training classes, which says no one can do your push ups for you. YOU are the only one who can choose how to live your life, and how to make it work. YOU have to decide and put into action the habit of taking 100% RESPONSIBILITY with close family and friends to create the positive relationships you want to enjoy.

Taking 100% Responsibility is a commitment. To YOU, to YOUR FAMILY and close friends. YOU have to ask for, expect and work for a return of that same commitment.

Look at your life, this very second, and decide, take responsibly for, the relationships you have. How does each one match up on a 0-10 basis…0 being the worst. What can YOU do to begin the process to make that relationship a 10.

One choice IS to be honest, stop blaming, stop feeling guilty, and give that relationship a vacation to make it a 10. Maybe some day you will look again and decide to change your evaluation and response and create a new value for 10. YOU do not get to say, well, it would be a 10 if he/she/they would "just" anything. This way of relating is also included in the Canfield Success Principles and specific classes offered from time to time around the world by trainers. Know the ask, and value to reach 10 as often as possible.

YOU have taken the RESPONSIBILITY to say and communicate, I am taking a vacation from this relationship because………….and fill in the blank that will bring it to 10. YOU have taken the RESPONSIBILITY to be vulnerable and open, honest and work on the issues as well as share what YOU need to bring that relationship to 10.

In close, vulnerable relationships, such as marriage, parents, siblings and children it is up to YOU to ask what YOU need to have a 10, then figure out if that is a relationship, or YOU just want everyone to do what YOU want at all times. This is a skill, and takes time, it is the push ups and the nutrition part of relationship skills and peace in the family. It is up to YOU at first to communicate how this can work and schedule time to allow it to become a strong, healthy way of life.

While choosing a program or method to reach 10 in all your relationships, YOU are choosing to stop blaming everyone else for why you do not have a 10 in relationships every day of your life. Joyce Meyer has a great talk about herself in which she was setting out on a cry fest, flung herself on her knees on the little rug by the toilet and cried demanding God fix everyone else. If "each one" would just see and do everything her way, how much more blessed life could be. She had what I call that God chat feeling, not "hearing" a voice but feeling it inside.......which said, its not them. She admits she was shocked, because there, on her prayer rug....no one else was near. She said to the voice "but no one else is here but me". "Exactly" prompted that inner voice.

Joyce has helped so many wives who know if their husbands would just give up watching sports on television, or going to games with "the guys", and stop playing golf, or going fishing, well, life would be grand. She has helped husbands, and parents in the same way.

She has spoken, and written lessons on the subject. An angry wife, or child, vacuuming the pile so hard it is coming off the carpet, or digging holes in the lawn by bitter mowing when they have to stay home to make YOUR day a 10 does not work.

A child sentenced to being grounded until their room is clean does not work. Instead have a discussion and sign a contract. YOU will leave the room, until its stink and piles sneak into the hallway....THEN you will go with trash bag and thrift store bag and clean that room. It is in the contract. YOU only have to clean it once and your child will get it. Usually that hoarding, stinking room is visited by a "friend" who is happy to go back to school and community and tell what a slob your child is. The message is received. The lesson learned. You and your child have enjoyed at least an 8 during the interim.

Many families have practiced "quiet five minutes" in free meditation classes at school. These work so well, the child often brings this home. A day started with a "quiet five minutes" instead of nagging, bickering, and chaos begins to improve the entire family experience as a weekly how are we doing dessert and half hour is added. These methods are taught in many family relationship programs and in the Canfield business principles book as well.

Little personal stories help show how this can work, within the family and with your own quiet time before you announce that if everyone else would just come up 9 points, YOU could enjoy a 10 family each and every day. I was injured in a vehicle accident and due to surgery and physical therapy I came to live with my older son. Every single day I woke up to being crabby and not taking responsibility for my own day, I admit, I let the little dog bowls sitting on the kitchen floor, ruin my day. My older son left fo work long before I got up. He made his own coffee, and shared a morning ritual with the dogs of a splash of half and half in their bowls. Off he went to work happy and a 10 with his pack.

Up I got. quickly letting my day become a 1. Peeved and bitter, I wondered, who did he think I was, Cinderella??? Had to pick up those small bowls and wash them. OR fall over them, with my crutches or get them stuck in the wheels of my wheelchair. Then I took a take 100% Responsibility class. I realized how much time I wasted and positive energy I wasted fuming over those bowls. All but one of the dogs were my therapy dogs, retired out of our animal assisted programs when I got hit by drunks racing. As I looked at the BIG PICTURE, I saw and found it took me less than 2 minutes to pick up those bowls, wash them and have a great day without my own load of self pity and blame. I went to the sink every single morning to measure my daily water, take my thyroid pill and it took me less than 3 seconds to put those bowls in the sink to wash later after I ate breakfast. By changing my own attitude, I changed my relationship and had gratitude that my son treated all the dogs equally with his dog.

Another story is about my Mom. She managed to ruin every holiday. We had gotten used to her finding someone to pick a fight with, and go roaring off in her sports car, saying she was off to kill herself. I had decided to work all holidays as it was usually triple time, and she often managed to get through a meal and be driven home without me. Yet, from time to time she still had her tantrums and stomped off, or demanded a ride home. I decided to ask her what she really wanted to do to be happy on holidays. She got mad and yelled, but finally admitted that the notorious "they" would think she was a "bad mother" and "bad grandmother" if she did not attend every holiday. She actually wanted to go visit with adult professional friends in formal meals and events. We said, let's give it a try. She went, she enjoyed, when she came home we invited her for left overs, or a lunch out and she told us all everyone was up to in their careers. No more ruined holidays. What would it take to make "a holiday" a 10 made her think and share. We all told her we did not care what "they" thought, it was none of "their" business.

This is the kind of relationship building anyone can learn in the ask how to make it a 10 regularly method of family building. It is a skill and takes learning and practice. Both to be vulnerable and honest, and to ask family members to be the same.

Working, learning and bringing PEACE to your own household, heart and relationships is a huge step forward in creating peace on earth. Think how great it could be if everyone started every day feeling loved, and calm and peaceful in a house that lived at 10 each day!. We can not control other families, friends, or relatives, but we CAN manage how we react to all in the family with stability and constant love. This can mean confrontation as conflict transformation training teaches. Conflict can mean honesty and transforming negative issues into solvable situations, instead of chaotic negative confrontations. The earlier we teach children and others this method of conflict resolving the better our own peaceful human development and design works, the more positive energy is built in the world.

COMMUNITY: HOW TO BUILD CONFLICT TRANSFORMATION IN YOUR LOCAL ENVIRONMENT: FRIENDS AND NEIGHBORS

Friends and Neighbors are the next step to building global peaceful human development and designing how to make it work for us in larger circles.

Build a neighborhood watch group. Start with the idea that we ALL need to help each other. This is not a cops and robbers game of "gotcha" and "punishment" and "wait 'til you see what 'THEY' are going to do to YOU game many people at workplaces, and in community groups love to play.

If you Google The United States Institute of Peace, and email what you are expecting to accomplish, they will guide you to often FREE online classes in mediation and community building no matter where you live. You can make it a point to ask one of the neighbors that may need help to fit in, to be part of the leadership team, and suggest that your neighborhood will create a pilot and teach the neighborhoods to build their own programs. There are many International colleges and universities that can be asked to provide this type of pilot model by asking their graduate students to assist your group for their research project. Many graduate students are expected to fundraise and build programs they can check back on four times a year to survey and provide data for a program being used to create research paper level work to graduate. They help your group for FREE. Public Administration, Charitable Project Administration,

Political Science and Education as well as Psychology graduate students are attached to professors, and networks of local professionals interested in creating safer, more peaceful neighborhoods. Many Scouts building their final projects need to research, design, and fundraise a community project to finish their final badge.

If you have a neighborhood watch, expand and make it best to serve your neighborhood.

Look at where you live, what are the needs?

Many neighborhoods are not well mixed. Many are still close. Others are mostly rentals, often college students. The constant change can create cold, and unsafe neighborhoods. If necessary find a community, religious or public building (libraries often have a conference room). Small restaurants often will let community groups that help the neighborhood meet for one or two hours between peak times. This helps family owned restaurants because meetings often lead to both take out and dine in eating, and new people learning about their food and what they offer. As local residents grow to respect and love the owners of the small businesses, and learn to respect one another, it lessens the violent crime. As residents become members of the neighborhood, instead of problems TO the neighborhood, the community grows, and is safer.

A suggestion is to send the persons best at making friends to homes that may be problems and ask them to be part of the leadership of the neighborhood. These, we have found, are often young veterans just out of service, and/or aged out foster youth, on the streets, or in college, but with no positive family support. When properly approached they quickly become a very valuable part of the neighborhood. Seniors, once in trouble themselves often have a connection with young neighborhood persons and include them as part of the solution rather than THE problem of the city.

I, as noted, like stories. A little old lady tells us of an area that was becoming unsafe. In her job she had to give out pay checks Saturday evenings to companies that were clients of her boss's private payroll service. She often brought a box of cash to cash checks for part time employees the company prepared and delivered checks to, as the part time, or new employees often had no bank accounts. One night she noticed a huge Hell's Angel's group had parked along the street, after that Saturday night, one or two of the bikers walked with her to deliver the checks and cash them, then walked her back to her car. She had always been nice to the part time workers, and some of the bikers noticed she could be in danger doing her job, and helping out the workers. So, they just leaned against their bikes and a couple escorted her. No one ever bothered her.

Working on a community project in gang and racially violent areas I asked the neighborhood Moms who had gang member children to introduce me to their gang member sons or daughters at a family event. One by one I met the gangsters, many I had seen in pictures posted on gang boards at the police and district attorney gang project offices within the areas they controlled. I do NOT recommend this for everyone. Mothers and OG past gangsters, now Grandfathers I did ask for help. Several gangsters I met in other situations. I helped out a family on Sundays, but due to my brain injuries from TSS was not driving, and had to take the bus. On Sundays, it was a three or four mile walk to the Grandmother's home where eight kids had to be home alone after church with the bedridden Grandmother. After dinner the Mom or Dad could drive me back up to a bus I could catch, that stopped across the street from my house.

I had watched a lovely vegetable garden grow over the months as I walked by. One day an arm was carefully caring for Middle Eastern cucumbers growing on stakes and rope frames. I said something about how amazing they were and my inability to ever get them to grow long enough to produce.

Each Sunday the arms and I would talk a moment. Sometimes I would be given a bag of cucumbers and other vegetables. Sometimes I would share a bag of horse poops from the stable where I boarded my equine therapy horses.

One day I was sitting at a bus bench when one of those awesomely painted, rock and walk vehicles came by. The gentleman in his bandana, jeans, tee shirt and flannel shirt asked if they could give me a lift. Sometimes one does not realize the danger of those who live in gangs. I said quite honestly that I had to work with ALL the gangs, and if seen riding in that undeniable and very identifiable vehicle, I could be seen as a danger and shot. He got it and was not offended that I did not accept a ride.

The cucumber man, I knew by then, from his picture on the Safe Streets wall of gangsters was a long term gangster, an OG, who had told me he was in process of retiring. Unlike movies, or gang tell alls, these gangsters often retired, many times during, or after long prison sentences, and being on parole, but were respected as OG members of the community.

I asked if he knew other OG retired gangsters who might help make the neighborhoods safer, and give at least the kids under 18 a chance they had not had in two hundred years. To get an education, find a dream and fill it.

Even I was a bit surprised to find that indeed the older, often retired gangsters helped communicate and mediate between gangs. I learned a lot more about gangs and gang systems which are covered in a book I will be publishing called "BIG LIZ, The Leader of the Gang" which is about the work I did for my Master's Degree in Bicultural Development Specialty, started in earlier days while working with young veterans returning from war who joined, or created a new type of gang from the old gangs based before World War I.

During a youth retreat at a private high school some years before, I had noted that some of the richest children not only belonged to gangster families, but also did not appear to be aware that this was an illegal way of life in America. I knew many of their parents from community and political groups I belonged to, or consulted for in community projects for my budding peace work.

While it was well known that many did not WANT peaceful cities, counties, states or nations, those children told us, in their innocent way WHY their parents were parts of what Peace classes teach in Peace Transformation are often called "spoilers". Negative forces that work against peaceful projects for their own interests rather than what is best for everyone.

It is necessary for any well intentioned community builders to acknowledge that some people just are against everyone living peacefully. It harms their own selfish goals. IF you learn to identify "spoilers" you will also need to learn to answer and address the "why" of them working against the process. A person who is just disinterested as opposed to a person who is working against the goals of peace and safety for all is the need to create a different, positive plan for reaching a positive goal.

Many projects that "work overnight" have been building for some time. Maybe years, maybe decades. The negatives that build an unsafe, unjust neighborhood may have taken years to develop. So many years, in fact, that the original goals, and problems are now just habitually accepted and followed because those that started them, and the reasons started may live long in the past.

ASK your initial group to work on the questions and suggest answers rather than YOU coming in to make it all YOUR way. We have found in this type of project that by asking the worst problem people to give us initial ideas and thoughts help to create a community resolution group, rather than a WE RIGHT, YOU WRONG continuum of the neighborhood issues.

When you ask college or graduate students to help facilitate the initial aspects of a project, you have people who have been educated in the HOW of creating a team. In business school it is taught that a group gets together, but must become a team to have true and sustainable success.

Identifying the most active people and most influencing (note NOT influential, influencing) people will be setting a list of those the neighborhood in initial interviews and your own observations is going to show YOU who needs to be addressed for positive change. Change is going to happen. Jack Canfield in his business work tells us that for a person or group to want change, they must have some idea of something better.

An example of this was apartments with babies and toddlers which it turned out had a seriously lacking disposal system. The Mothers with children had in city after city taken to the same habit, which was to toss used baby diapers out the windows in to the parking lot below. At the initial site, when asked to consult on changing the outcome, which was a privately owned parking lot, spaces rented out by the month to large office buildings in the area, getting constant complaints from their customers of dirty used baby diapers being splatted on and around their vehicles each day, a disgusting and truly unhealthy situation, we laughed. We ourselves had had NO experience with this problem until we did our observation.

A used baby diaper is filled with human excrement that STINKS. It also attracts rats, and birds that tear the plastic and inner material to EAT that excrement. This in turn leaves torn plastic, shredded material, and excrement, often glued together with greasy diaper rash and baby lotions on the cars in the parking lot below. It also spreads the excrement and makes it harder to clean off vehicles. and is tracked on shoe into offices and stores.

We can easily understand why people who paid to park while working would be upset and angry over the situation. Many a cursing shouting match had occurred when a driver actually saw a person toss a used diaper out the window of the multi-story apartment.

As we continued our observations, we realized this was not ONE apartment, or ONE situation. We found streets littered with these plastic bound nightmares that often washed into the drains, into the sewers and worse, into the river beds that ran down to the ocean. AND we found that while new, these conveniences were becoming a huge problem for the environment. This small neighborhood problem was an opportunity to get many together, to resolve issues, involve people in their own neighborhood, as well as become involved in global environmental resolutions.

Moving on in this one problem helped us to realize these were not slovenly people, they had issues they needed help to address successfully. This became a city issue. This will be addressed in the Chapter on peaceful human development and design of cities by citizens.

Schools and safety of children are something that need designing and ongoing attention to by every citizen. We need to constantly be THE PEOPLE that create our own schools and community. At least small children, in large cities, need to have busses. It is up to the parents to say THIS IS NOT WORKING and fix schools, not wait for an appointed person by a group of elected people to say what was relevant ten or more years ago needs to continue, or not. Bussing was supposed to make all schools equal it did not. Except that it made a lot more children and youth go to bad schools where education was not happening. Rich white as well as rich minorities moved (I was in high school when bussing and what was called "block busting" happened). They also put their kids in private schools. Over the years instead of a balance by ALL parents creating better, safer schools for ALL, charter, and public privatized schools as well as "star" programs were designed and paid for, and poverty area students were bussed to schools too far for their parents to deal with or be involved with. No one likes to say bussing did not work, because at least more attention came to the issues of racism and classism in America.

Now is the time for each community to get involved and make all schools work. The same book, with what teachers call "the school police" did NOT work. During COVID children did not LIKE the computerized programs. ASK the students at all levels why, and fix them. ASK the parents why and fix them. ASK the teachers why, and fix that.

Sitting at church some years back Reverend Jessie Jackson was speaking, he had been sitting next to me, what a nice man, concerned about children, about parents working hard and not getting the American promised benefits, or UN promised benefits for themselves, or their children. We must read his work, and writings of many others to realize poor white children for twenty years at that time, were not just not getting an education a chance to dream, support for those dreams, they were getting beaten up and accused of racism by minority children of all backgrounds. The rich white kids went to private schools, all middle class children whose parents could afford it, sent their kids to private schools as well. A small number of parents fooled themselves and others by creating public schools, that in fact were private schools at taxpayer expense.

Everyone was shocked to hear that while Black students had their own school, they were not provided with a library, Rain, snow or blow as the old saying goes, he and many others waited outside the back door of the public library, paid for with tax payers money (ALL their parents paid taxes)in case the librarian "might" decide to come and ask them if they wanted a book. And decide if she was going to let them have the one requested.)WE do not teach this reality to any of the children we bring up to believe reading is bad and as one student told me, just another way whites are keeping minorities down. Being brown, I spoke to his parents, in front of him about this misconception of hate. Even he did not mention that Native American children were at the time of his school days, not allowed in public schools, Black separate schools, or small church run schools for migratory Latino children. Teens of all minorities, and poverty level whites were expected to quit school and go to work to help support the family. This is not taught either. Middle class teens all worked in family business or found jobs around town, or at farms of family to earn money for college and things they wanted, not needed. Cars, more expensive clothing were NOT something parents were EXPECTED to provide. Certainly not college! Many doctors, lawyers, business people were veterans, used their vet-education money to help with college, and worked waiting tables, cleaning at night, or driving taxi to get through.

It is important as a community to teach children that "getting" every THING YOU want is not anyone's job, not even yours. In a structured program for high risk families, we ASKED the State Children's Protection lawmakers to tell us exactly what children and teens WERE legally required to be provided. It was JUDGES and POLICE that asked. Nutritional food was broken down to one vitamin pill, and three servings of low sugar, high protein cereal with canned milk each day. A sleeping bag on the floor was considered to NOT be neglect. As long as the clothing was warm, or cool as weather dictated, it was adequate.

One little girl had demanded some THING or other from her Grandmother who had taken custody when asked by the Court. Both her parents were in prison. When the Grandmother told her no, the child began to be abusive and demanded to know why. The Grandmother said no money. The child said, well put your card in, and get some. Her Grandmother explained you have to put money in to get money out. No one had explained that to the child before. It is ALL of our responsibility to know and to teach that in order to have money, we have to put some in. Some of the richest people and politicians have not learned this, they think if others put in the money, they should have it. (isn't that a robber mentality). Many of our students in high risk single parent programs had arrogantly told teachers they did not need an education, they would have a baby and get welfare.

No one had bothered to tell them it is not easy to actually live, not just exist, on welfare.

We all need to look at the past, look at now, and look at what we can do to help the earth, nature and all people live better lives to leave the world better and more thankful than we found it when born. This is building community. In the past, town was community, today people move so often, we have to create community and uphold it for ALL. Robbery and stealing from people at work, school, or in our community are all the same as stealing from family. Sadly, some people think that is OK as well. Building community starts with admitting these problems all exist and working together to stop the problems.

CITY: BUILDING PEACE IN EACH CITY BY CITIZENS

Yesterday, two groups of teens were violent and misbehaving at a huge amusement park. The police were called. Everyone had to leave the park. Many people had saved, and looked forward to spending that day at that amusement park. Many families and seniors from the area go to dinner there, just for the food and to take pies home. They look forward to it.

Because of a few rotten kids, everyone lost a nice evening. No charges were filed. In other instances bored teens texted a time and place and rushed in and mob robbed stores. They all were gone when police arrived. BUT, there are schools nearby and the store video easily identified every singe youth. No charges filed. We as a nation have gotten in the habit of letting rotten people of all ages ruin everything. It is time to say NO loudly and put a stop to it. It needs to be stopped at schools, and it is time to admit schools are just what one child wrote to President Bush in 2001. These are just places where the rotten kids hurt everyone and the teachers yell at the rotten kids and " NO ONE CARES". The President cared, wrote back and started a program called "no kid left behind". As fast as possible, the corrupt managed to take the money, NOT use it to improve schools for any kids, and things got worse. We need oversight, and for God's sake, foresight.

CITIES need to have parents together with police, school and citizens to raise good kids. We created programs WITH the kids, both kids who behaved and those who did not.

WE NEED a school nurse (at least one for every 300 children in a school, and interns who are single working parents going to medical or nursing school can add the additional hours PAYING for the units they get while learning and helping). We can easily ask the biggest HMO s and nursing schools to help with these projects. THEY get a tax exemption, and good publicity and give their employees a great break from the day to day, and help train new hires about their real job. (hint, not the paperwork).

As discussed in this book, people want to know WHY America is such a goal point, yet many, if not most people do NOT consider the WHY and fix their own communities and countries. Eleanor Roosevelt had this in mind when she formulated her goals for the UN. Rather than what it has become, the UN was expected by the First Lady to become a way for people around the globe to BE in their own local cities what THEY wanted, which number one was FREE, and second SAFE. People come to America and work HARD to make their dreams come true, and deserve America to stand behind equality and justice for everyone. This does NOT mean American taxpayers money and/or American troops get involved. It does not mean immigrants come and think Americans are all rich and can and should let them break laws, and start businesses against ordinances that keep Americans from starting and running local businesses.

This starts in our cities. Many changes in the law were made to allow and to protect small sidewalk businesses owned and operated by both citizens and immigrants to help ease the problems for all. Many health department inspectors were accused of being racist. In fact, they found live rabbits and other animals (some picked up at the park, chipped and with owners) being slaughtered in kitchens, and kept in cages in the stockrooms, being sold as "chicken".

While in other countries people may have had a small fire, and cooked any animals unlucky enough to wander by after being brined and hot peppered so much no one realizes what they are eating, or that it is not refrigerated while in brine, it is unhealthy and illegal in America for push carts, caterers, and restaurants to serve either road kill, or illegally grabbed strays. While rabbit MAY be honestly sold on menus, it can NOT be kept in backrooms, breeding and spreading excrement in a food environment. And no animal is allowed to be slaughtered in food carts, restaurants, or backyard illegal breeding cages.

I have used food as an example of problems that separate citizens from immigrants because it is easy to see why the laws need to apply to everyone. Food is NOT the only place the laws of a nation need to be regarded and honored by all. Bringing in undeclared money and using it to fund illegal businesses until big enough to buy legal businesses, then saying Americans are too lazy to be successful is not OK.

IF the government wants to use taxpayers money to give refugees advantages taxpayers do NOT get, voters NEED to make sure they want that, and let legislators know. It is NOT that taxpayers are stingy, but when they can not afford a home, or business, partly because they pay high rent and high taxes, they become upset about their money being used to help others get above them financially, and then demean them for being too lazy or spendthrift to create their own benefits. This is a problem in welfare programs as well. While out doing surveys about citizens infighting, one major issue listed was taxpayers doing without, due to high taxes in all areas, while people who did not work got benefits the taxpayers could not afford.

Sensitivity and understanding what people believe is part of inclusion and helping your community become a better village for everyone. By listening to everyone and by facilitating for everyone to LISTEN to each other equally is NOT taking one side or the other. It is helping them communicate and understand one another and build peaceful resolution to issues. This does NOT mean compromise, it MAY mean to learn to be able to say, and feel that its OK to disagree without being disagreeable. (Supreme Court Justice Ruth Bader/Ginsberg's favorite admonition to all).

While teaching at the UN schools I was trained to find a way to interject the material we were taught with age appropriate games, discussions, etc. I chose a small toy village that could be compared to another toy that could be manipulated to present each person, house, business, item as unique and yet work together.

If we truly want a community that is equal and justice for each person, we need to understand this means, we are NOT all perfectly all the same. I used the small toys, shaped like eggs, to help get discussions going in ALL age groups, whether teachers, other educators, community leaders such as police, judges, fire fighters, politicians and religious leadership. Men and women, and of course children, who always understood quickly and perfectly.

Ask yourself, what is the first thing people do when confronted with developments of similar housing. They begin to add changes. I was animal sitting for a friend who lived in a new development, I let her off at the shuttle and returned to her house. Each of maybe thirty huge intersections looked exactly the same! By the time I was able to reach her by phone, she told me which street to turn left, then which to turn on and the number. I STILL had trouble finding her home! I had been there many times, but was NOT driving and had not noticed how similar each cul-de-sac and street was.

By the street and house number, my GPS on my phone I finally found this amazing and unique, but not at all unique house! We want things similar, do we all really want to be just copies of everyone else??

Loving and honoring community is the first step to making a working city. This does NOT mean allow people to harm others in any way!

Taking a mediation class, or reading mediation books and learning online for free, you can learn how to talk to people to stay OUT of disputes, yet help people either resolve issues, or agree to disagree.

After a school board meeting, or city hall meeting when people have been disrespected and shoved aside with a rote "thanks for your thoughts", you can ask people to meet and talk about what CAN be done, not what gets ignored. As discussed in the Chapter on Community, there are usually places available to meet, Small sidewalk coffee shops, the park for a snack, and beverage while the kids play. Out in front of the school after dropping off the children. On a rainy, or hot day, meeting on a long bus ride across town and back, and chatting is informal and gives everyone a chance to say what they have to say. In the rules of mediation, each gets to talk, then passes the item used to move on to the next person. These are called HEART TALKS, and were a big part of community and family building mediation programs in the late 1900's in America. The original pass item was a soft red heart glued to a stick, or tongue depressor, and passed as each person had a turn. The details of heart talks are online, and in Jack Canfield classes.

Now that you have built even TWO families in community, it is time to build a city involved group. (As you grow and include, you will include almost everyone. Little old people, disabled people, single parents of disabled children are home and feel excluded, can be amazing parts of community by making phone and internet contacts which helps all BE INCLUDED.

Some of those who cause the problems, when you have skills to approach them, can be included and become a great asset in the community. There are classes in inclusion and building community at many colleges and at the Peace Universities and Academies all over the world. USInstitute of Peace has listings of these programs and Academies on their web site.

Families often have no idea of how to get help for distressed and distressing relatives. Small community groups can find out the best ways to deal and get help from those PAID to deal with troublesome family members, and/or neighbors. By having small community groups that DO know how to get help, they also can help other small community groups spread the word about problems and how to get help locally.

Small inclusive community groups also help ALL members of a city, county and State, as well as Congressional and Senate elections to be discussed with local, knowledgeable people so everyone can legally vote, become citizens, and take part in elections intelligently, not just following the most trendy hate filled commercials to vote for representation in all areas.

COUNTY: EDUCATING FOR PEACE

Most counties came into being from clusters of cities, from rural farmers and small towns joining together to fight off cities, or groups that had more money and destroyed the ability to live peaceably in their own homes and lands of thousands. In later years of the 20th century, counties began to rise out of clustered, crowded cities that joined in certain goals.

As each city comes together, it is time to start learning about your county and who and why it is run the way it is. Thomas Jefferson, among others, had a vision of PEOPLE living in local areas, by their own local regulation, yet bound by the principles and commitments of the Constitution. Some of the founders were just wanting to get away from the taxes and overrun by the elite of the countries they had left. Some of the founders wanted more equality, better justice systems, but did NOT embrace equality of all. Some of the founders truly embraced the vision of a government OF the People, BY the People and FOR the People in order for peace, justice and liberty to become a wholesome, new vision for all.

READ the Declaration of Independence, and the Constitution, you can find both online, or get a free copy in the office of your Congresspersons and Senators. These are both short, easily read documents. The discrepancies between the beliefs of those creating the documents of the new nation are glaring and obvious, yet, over two hundred years, Americans have worked and even had civil wars and armed disruptions to gain those rights for more people.

In the courses listed in many Universities and Colleges, and international peace academies you can find classes that train people to become active and responsible as well as to include all people in any city, county, state or nation in the resolution of issues that lead to hate, division, and violence.

In a county it is necessary to find out what that county is actually responsible for in your State. Not all are the same. While most cities have fire, paramedic, police and education as well as large infrastructure such as water, energy, the modern modality has led to income tax, state tax, and property as well as sales taxes being divided by higher governance, which has led to people often paying for services that are not authorized, or responsible to the local taxpayers and voters.

The County is responsible for groups of cities, to make sure they are getting the money appropriated for them, and paid by their taxes. Another county responsibility is to make sure the RIGHTS of taxpayers and voters are upheld, in particular over foreign interests, and out of state interests. This duty has slid away over decades, but the citizens and taxpayers can utilize mediation and elections to return these protections of rights to the citizen. What this means in your particular county is for you to find out and make sure citizens know when elections are upcoming.

Most, if not all states have increasingly hard to understand port, airport, transportation appropriations and rights. In states with legal gambling, legal sales of drugs, and other highly taxed activities it is necessary that each county Board be responsible and knowledgeable about what money is due, how much the county has a right to, what it is to be spent for, and to make sure each State is accountable for any money due the county from these sources. Small family farm communities would surely NOT vote to have water rated increased, while they can not grow a few vegetables, or have been told to cut showers to 30 seconds so out of state and foreign factory farms get more water and bring in illegal labor trafficked humans who often steal from local homes and businesses because they have nowhere to live, no good clothing and. little food. Today most food banks demand ID, and only give families a once a month box of food. Illegal labor is not welcome.

The County of San Bernardino, in the State of CA by its County Supervisors Board has made the announcement that if the State does not do the oversight and transparency needed, the County will secede from the State and apply to be the 51st State of the United States. Their stated reason is that through improper oversight and transparency this County is not being paid Federal, or State income needed to take care of the citizens, and that the State puts in restrictions and regulations that make it more expensive and less viable for the County to meet obligations to taxpayers.

In the news conference the Board made it clear this is not what they want to do, but it is their duty to protect the taxpayers and all others in San Bernardino, even if in reality that means to protect them from the State of California. (ABC news, 7 Los Angeles, July 27, 2022).

I have added this story into this book to show that elected officials can and do take their responsibility to those that elect and pay them seriously. This particular story shows, through the mid-line, rather than hate filled, or aggressive approach to the issues that the Board is hearing the citizens, has analyzed and attempted to resolve the issues, and is now stepping up the representation within the laws, to represent the concerns and rights of their voters and taxpayers.

STATE: EDUCATING FOR INCLUSION AND PEACE

Where does YOUR State come from??? Only now are States, the USA and the world beginning to deal with the systemic genocide that even the Bible sanctions in the earliest of biblical recorded history.

In the early part of the 1400's guns were invented. Shortly thereafter used for warfare. It is necessary for ALL humans to go backward in time and establish a clear picture of their own local reality, not the historical myths spread through education over the centuries.

The United Nations Charter guarantees that all member countries will honor the right of PEOPLE to BELONG somewhere and to not have those rights to "somewhere" taken from them by better armed countries. In general saying. "civil war" and calling the native people "insergents" makes them the wrong people, rather than the wronged people. This goes on in States as well.

The reality of this right comes with the responsibility of each local area, and STATE making this a reality. Some people BELONG there, others came in many ways, and now have nowhere else to BELONG. It is going to take work to figure out how that works in each STATE, let alone each nation and the almost 200 nations of the world.

It is going to take a historic look at reality, not made up "we are great" myths made up by what in the greatest parts of history have been genocides by one race usually justified by the Bob Dylan mentioned "God on OUR side" gang. (Bob Dylan "With God on Our Side).

Those who tried to stay alive, or thought to make a big buck by going along with the ones who did the killing and maiming by tricking or threatening youngsters, or building up a big "hero" myth and clothes and food for starving kids to make them sign up for the next big "victory"….need to look at reality and make sure no teen, or young person EVER falls for that again. Buffy Sainte Marie told us plainly in her song, Universal Soldier, that it is no longer the distant "they" that keeps war going. It is you and me, by our votes, our taxes and the blood and sanity of our young people.

NATION

Joining together with people in your nation may be very different. America has 50 States, and additional territories that can NOT declare or participate in war, or keep its own military. Each of them has, at this point in time, extreme corruption and crime. Each one is allowed State Marshalls and guards as well as county and local police. Many states have civil conflict within their borders with police and citizen issues. But what is the worst threat to most people? Drunk and reckless drivers, and people who think they are the mythical Robin Hood if they break the law and commit crimes.

Does any criminal really think it is the same to shoot an unarmed man on his way to work who unfortunately stopped at the wrong gas station to get gas for the day as to take part in taking food from the one or two monarchs or despots who take ALL the food and earnings for their family enjoyment and leave the rest of the population to work as slaves and to live in poverty. Many seem to.

Drugs. Both the extreme expense of medicine and medications for the middle, working, taxpaying America and street drugs. One of the top three causes of death, either from the drugs or the criminals that sell them.

Hate:

In America in particular, but almost all, if not all, nations in the world the residents live divided and hate filled, fed to all by media and political games.

It is important for each and every RESIDENT to determine what their nation is about, and then decide how to address that reality in view of the Charter of the United Nations. The Ten Rights and

Responsibilities of the United Nations give every person on earth rights, by expecting those rights, each person on earth needs to expect of themselves and be expected by others to give the responsibilities to every other person on earth. that go along with each right.

Groups of residents have every right to go to the United Nations and ask for advice on how to work together in their nation. Again, the warning and reality of "spoilers" is essential. Professional Peace builders can be requested to help in non-violent conflict resolution to work WITH and inclusively with ALL residents of your nation. Contacting local Universities and Colleges may help you find conflict transformation students and Professors who can assist any citizen group learn the basic to INCLUDE everyone in resolving conflicts for sustainable results.

INTERNATIONAL

International, or between nation conflict need to be addressed by the TWO nations with conjoining borders, ONLY. The UN has peacekeeping councils, and peace builders. These issues need to be addressed there, withOUT the financial, for political interference of other nations. The UN needs to be well known to ALL world citizens, from the history of the intent by Eleanor Roosevelt and others, to remove international aspects of war. The War to End War, World War II was supposed to be the last war that utilized violence around the world.

Today, of course a nation OFTEN sends money, weapons, and interfere in conflict within nations or with their neighboring bordered nations. It is up to the HUMANS to make sure their own country (especially America since the Constitution prohibits ANY involvement in conflicts of other nations except by diplomacy and boycotts, or refusal to give American citizens travel, work, or education Visas to those countries until the risk of violent conflict may put Americans at risk!) stays out of conflict between nations that could lead the nuclear armed nations into what WILL be the last war. The fifties. Nuclear War Treaties and Bans, and the work of President JFK were all based on the real scientific work proving there could be no such thing as "limited" nuclear war, and the movie War Games made forty years later, was a true depiction of what science proved more and more over the decades.

If we look to history, we find that George Washington himself, as President, wanted to have a Peace Agency, with balanced power to the War Agency, and to maintain both as integral information agencies for Congress, the President and even the Supreme Court to gain information BEFORE involving America in armed conflicts that were NOT dealing with a threat from bordering countries to the United States of America itself.

He was over ridden by spoilers.

Today we do have International laws and courts. They often are ignored by countries, even those supposedly strong members and supporters of the UN.

International courts need to be cleaned and respectable so they can be respected.

GLOBAL

As Space exploration and capability for space stations, and growth of violent conflict grows, it is necessary to improve and strengthen global peace laws and enforcement of those laws.

Global peace is beyond conflict within nations, or conflict between nations. It is up to ALL humans to learn and live by the regulations of the United Nations Charter to limit and deal non-violently with conflict around the world.

Each human needs to learn and respect the reality of the bombing of Hiroshima and the Nuclear War threat and treaties of the fifties and sixties.

It is my personal belief that when we as humans obtained the capacity to destroy every living thing on earth for seventy years, seventy times over, we as humans had made war obsolete. The tiniest, just born baby would be 70 when able to safely go out of a radiation proof chamber, if in fact there was such a thing, and somehow had managed to put 70 years plus, of food, water and supplies in that chamber BEFORE the five minutes or less it would take to sentence nature and the entire life of the globe to death.

A United States General speaking in Pasadena about the safety of our "bomb shelters" told a crowd of citizens, police, doctors and scientists that we were fortunate, in an all out nuclear war, we were considered "first strike" and would be gone, dust, in less than a minute. Others might last two or three weeks as they died of starvation, bad water, dead air, dead water and civil wars over the last few bits of food and water, until all was finally at peace on the earth for an estimated 70 years. The movie "WAR GAMES" shows a credible expectation of a world nuclear war. The computer tells us in the end that like Tic Tac Toe, Thermo-nuclear war is a game that no one can win. The best strategy is not to play.

To play a continuum of small "not wars", we are told they are advisory, or police actions, helping others is equally without support, if in fact war is obsolete. What is the purpose of killing people a few at a time (thousands?) when the reasons can be worked out. If in fact the real reasons are ever admitted honestly.

An amazing statement of President Eisenhower is contained in his final speech to the nation. A General that warned us against war. The final address to the nation can be found online, or a copy found in the National Archives of Presidential speeches.

We find that President George Washington asked for a Department of Peace, and rejected the idea of "empire building" either for America, or for any other nation. The autobiographical journals, letters and articles about Washington let us know he, among others recognized the dangerous idea of making America into a growing and corrupt mega-government, but instead a small, locally formed government to maintain equal rights and justice. The FACT that even Washington and others left out the Natives that owned the lands, and the slaves and indentured persons brought from all over the world to do the hard work, does NOT negate the principle and ideal of peace, equality and justice for ALL, which in FACT the Constitution has over the 200 plus years expanded to include most people.

In the years since America was founded, it has grown, the ideals and principles have been hard won for every person on American soils. This has been abused in some ways to TAKE away rights from many. WE are the ones who must each day make sure the rights are for everyONE, and be a role model for other countries. As related to GLOBAL rights, we ALL have to work at accepting and standing up for the rights of every person globally to live a free and just life, and many around the world are going to have to learn to share THEIR ideals and principles, but NOT use violent conflict to make EVERYONE do as they want.

The hardest thing for anyone to accept is THEY MIGHT BE WRONG, or that THEIR idea of what is right for someone else is not their business….and yet, at what point DO we stand up for those not being given rights, or having their rights taken by violence of power, money, physical harm and conflict means. Even if we do not agree with them, if we fail to stand up for others right to live FREE and themselves, it will one day circle around to where we ourselves find we are the ones on the gossip circuit of a media that feels it has the right to force it's ideas on everyone.

Yet WE are the ones who can stop it immediately by not listening, not buying the products that support them, and making sure the advertisers know we are not going to buy their products until media and journalism is free all over the world.

In each area, from our own standing up to and for ourselves and others to standing up for global rights of all, we will create more peace on earth. Many people are surprised to find out it is one person at a time expecting and standing up for equal rights and justice for ALL that will lead to their own having less of their own rights and equality gone.

There is an old saying a friend of mine brought from his own childhood, that saying is "if you are not nice enough to be nice, be smart enough". This saying is presented to children in many forms, but in essence teaches us that even if we are not kind and nice enough to stand up for others, make sure when we get a chance to be nice because the next person needing rights or kindness might be we, ourselves.

The rights we have not stood up for to help others, might be lacking when we ourselves need them. Another point is, you may yell at someone, and when you get to the bus and forgot your wallet, or call a plumber as your house fills with water….or come to a court, find the person you yelled at in charge!!! God bless.

This does not mean not to stand up firmly for your own rights and those of others at all times. Wimpy is not nice. To yourself or others. One of the greatest, most successful ways I have found to get people to stand up for what is right is to ask them for advice, and help on how to accomplish what is needed. One of my stories is when I decided someone had to stand up and ask the gangs and criminals to stop ruining the future for their own children and young relatives, and destroying the lives of their elderly and disabled family members, I went to the gangs and asked them how that might look, how we could all work together, and safely accomplish a chance for kids to grow, and elders to grow old in peace in their own neighborhoods.

In that work, we did not officiously go in and demand the gang members stop selling drugs or running rackets in prostitution and gambling. We DID ask them what their children might have a chance to be if given that chance in neighborhoods not lovingly called "the casbah" areas in which rich white men went to do things they would never have allowed in the neighborhoods they, their daughters and wives had to live in.

Globally, corruption and crime are the two greatest threats to all, while nuclear war is greater, environmental destruction and the greed of corporations over the rights of ALL humans and NATURE herself create these horrors.

One by one, corporations have started to join environmental positive projects and reduce, or eliminate their carbon, toxic and human suffering footprint on the neck of nature and the world itself. Each of us has the ability to not purchase products, to urge environmental good citizenship and stop human and animal trafficking forever. Stop buying products from, investing in, and supporting any corporation that does not have the best interests of every human, animal and the planet in mind in all they do.

As discussed in earlier chapters there are those called "spoilers" that will NOT become part of any peace growing, or good for everyone and everything attempt. As peace builders it is important to be honest with yourself, your group, and without hate or bitterness figure out the who and why of the spoilers involved in any global (or local project or goal).

It is easy to find many spoilers because no matter what anyone has to say that is honest, positive and in the best interest of all, that person or group will attempt to bring hate and division into the discussions and meetings.

WHO is doing the spoiling???

Sometimes spoiling is someone well hidden behind lawyers, CEO's and in another country. It might be paid violent people. It might be paid politicians or their workers. When your group finds out WHO is the spoiler and who is doing the spoiling and how that spoiling is playing out, it is time to talk, and design a way to go around the spoilers. From a member of your own family, even possibly yourself in personal issues (self sabotage in diet, school, saving for something worthwhile, addictions) it is important to know the WHO, HOW and WHY of spoilers to eliminate or reduce the effect of their antics on working to make positive change. Globally, every single person needs to take part in at least one project and work to make peace and restoration of the earth, ocean, air, forests and animals, as well as the 10 rights and responsibilities of every human come to be real, for ALL.

One of the most important issues in Global peace building is honesty, transparency and oversight on both projects, and spending with severe global penalties for anyone involved in Global corruption and interference with the rights of every person and every nation on earth.

Oversight as discussed in previous chapters is possible, easily and consistently, but is ignored and overwhelmed with bureaucracy and failure to follow through. Every day computers make oversight, and transparency easier, and less costly. Computers are finally being put to the uses they were meant for, to pass information at super speeds, and make it harder and harder for corrupt for illegal activities to occur.

An important part of Global peace is health. The United Nations has huge international networks of health agencies, yet COVID, and now Monkey Pox have over run the world. Hundreds of millions of dollars are donated by America alone to establish and oversee health in the world. Yet both of these diseases have become pandemic. HIV/AIDS among others before these. E Coli, says French news, is an easily prevented disease, an easily controlled disease, and NOT an easily cured disease.

How many from nations considered technical and health controlled know that just good sewage systems and bleach can eliminate E. coli??? Has anyone done a study of the COVID precautions to find out if E. Coli and HIV/AIDS both reduced in occurrence due to the increased bacterial, fungal, and viral warnings to avoid the disease COVID???

Fifty years ago, as the UN unfurled its new wings, the world health organizers worked WITH countries to identify and limit contamination by foods and products from one country to others, wanting to quickly identify and curb global pandemics. Children in many countries took small orange boxes out trick-or-treating to raise the one penny, nickels, and dimes that could vaccinate everyone in other counties and reduce many serious diseases. Ticks, fleas, mosquitoes were controlled, sewage systems researched and implemented, research done to create better sewage and trash disposal in ALL nations to limit spread of diseases. Why is this not practiced today when both humans and products move quickly and freely about the world??? It would seem, in open, honest evaluation that no one could be found that did not think the health of everyone on earth was more important than stealing the funds for humane purposes. That sadly is not true.

The orange boxes are reduced to only one or two countries, and very limited in use. The orange boxes, even in the most poverty stricken nations, where a school might only raise one hundred pennies did in fact learn about disease, prevention, and hope!

Each of us can join in our block, city and county, state and nations and start the Orange Box charitable programs again, with local oversight. To facilitate children and teens learning how to raise money, one penny at a time, and give to save lives around the world, as well as how to keep positive measures going globally without anything but world health in mind.

This would give a positive project for the smallest child, to every teen to be part of the world, and make it a better place. This project spread "sister city" projects around the world in which children and parents of classrooms partner up with other classrooms across the world and share many unifying communications and help for one another.

This project can be added to recycling and environmental clean up projects of whole groups, communities and cities. Engineering students at every engineering institute and technical program in the world have to create projects to graduate. Scouts, and other youth programs require community service and later complete community service projects to gain their top awards. Put these together.

Ask community groups to donate money, and ask restaurants, stores, and wholesalers to give you the best prices possible on cartons of snacks, and water for each project. AND REMEMBER TO RECYCLE the containers!

What does this have to do with peace???

When nature herself is being healed and restored, we will ALL feel positive energy flowing and be happier, better people.

When we are part of something big, by doing something small…..plant five dwarf fruit trees and a small container garden at your home, or at your child's school, or a local nursing or independent senior living complex and dedicate them to "Trees for Jane" the Jane Goodall project. Donate to local Native Nations projects such as the Forests and Meadows projects of the Leonard Peltier Foundation. In one project you have helped people help nature, clean the air, help be part of the solution to environmental issues, and helped one of the world's most inspiring and great women help wild animals keep their homes and lives. Helped one of the greatest Native leaders who said, Natives are people, in fact the owners and caretakers of these lands in his projects to restore and rebalance nature. And best of all, selfishly, you have made yourself feel like we CAN salvage our world. One plant, one tree, one person at a time. If your project raises money to buy the trees and plants by cleaning up your own block and one block of local area that needs cleaning......how much greater we all feel!

AND YOU can find or build a new project once a month! Or once a week!

Many projects you can be part of at the last moment, go buy a shirt, walk along with people, bring your wheelchair, push a friend or family member in their wheelchair, bring your crutches and your little wheelie so you can stop and sit as needed. Even large and long events need people to sit, smile, encourage everyone, at water stops along the way!!!

Many projects have booths, find some others to go and listen to the speakers, and make the round of the booths. Bring your community group, at least once a month together to learn and support those making a difference.

Schools used to have little booths and fun. Create something with teachers and get sponsors to bring booths. You will be surprised at how happy the librarian is to host weekly evening or Saturday reading events. Four or five families can host just one two-hour event a YEAR and support the library. College students and IT employees of big corporations can come and share their skills and teach us all how to better interface our computers with hard copy books and magazines at the library to know more about areas of more interest to each member of the community.

Computers are wonderful tools, many books can be found and read online, but curling up in a family ball with pets and reading books together is just better. We can learn to respect and use computers and books.

Bring one, leave one book exchanges can be hosted by just ONE classroom a month in the school library. The Parents group can raise money and three times a year have snacks and waters, often obtained at huge discount from area stores and restaurants, or wholesalers to introduce their items and hand out cards to introduce all the families to their stores or restaurants. Big wholesale children's book companies often will send a bookmobile of low priced popular books and help raise money and books for the library, foster and children's hospital art and occupational therapy rooms!

It is always a good opportunity for local bus services to give a four hour free bus ride to the event and back to limit traffic and parking problems, and it costs the city a lot less than additional traffic police for the traffic it reduces. Families that are less likely to attend can be asked early to help host the event. This creates inclusion, and helps all be part of the school and community. When each village, community and city begin small, it will spread to the whole earth.

Learning together as a world is fun, and will help each of us take a lead in peace building around the world.

CLOSING

In closing, each area of this book is an area you can find one or more ways to make the world better that is easy and often is just YOU making up your mind, to believe and live peace, no matter what the rest of the world is doing.

As an example, I have worked for many areas of peace for decades, some projects I worked on, invented, or volunteered to help are today amazing examples of just thinking, praying and believing bringing a tiny bit more peace and balance to this world. Many times I am so sweetly surprised that others have grabbed an idea, or listened in a conference and come home to make their world a better place! That action inspired others and the ideas and better world grew!

Many believers of all back grounds over centuries, over thousands of years have found that a job too big, too scary for one person, done in tiny parts by many is successful! Peace.

Printed in the United States
by Baker & Taylor Publisher Services